FIGURES IN CHINA'S SPACE INDUSTRY

Who is Tu Shou'e?

By Ye Qiang and Dong Pingping

Books Beyond Boundaries

ROYAL COLLINS

Tu Shou'e was only a child when the Japanese army bombed Shanghai during World War II, but the war left a deep and lasting scar on his heart. A blitz of shells were dropped by roaring enemy planes, and completely destroyed the once bustling city. The war urged the boy to closely tie his future with the fate of his country.

3

Later, Tu Shou'e went to the Massachusetts Institute of Technology (MIT) to study aeronautics. He was determined to build an aircraft for China so that his country could be strong and prosperous.

In 1945, Japan surrendered. Tu Shou'e was excited when he heard the news. After the war, thinking that his beloved country lay in ruins, Tu quit his job and returned to China to contribute to her reconstruction.

In February 1957, Tu Shou'e received an offer to study missiles at the Fifth Research Institute of the Ministry of National Defense. In the beginning, Tu and his colleagues had almost no material support in collecting data and carrying out experiments. They started everything from scratch. In September 1957, Tu negotiated with the Soviet Union as an adviser to the Chinese government delegation. They reached an agreement on the introduction of missile technology. Tu's dream of "making China's own missiles" was about to come true.

However, just as the team was making progress on the project, the Soviet Union suddenly broke the contract and withdrew all experts and all research materials. The missile development project was forced to a halt without completion: the Chinese scientists fell into a dilemma.

Should they give up? Should they continue? Or should they wait for another opportunity to show up?

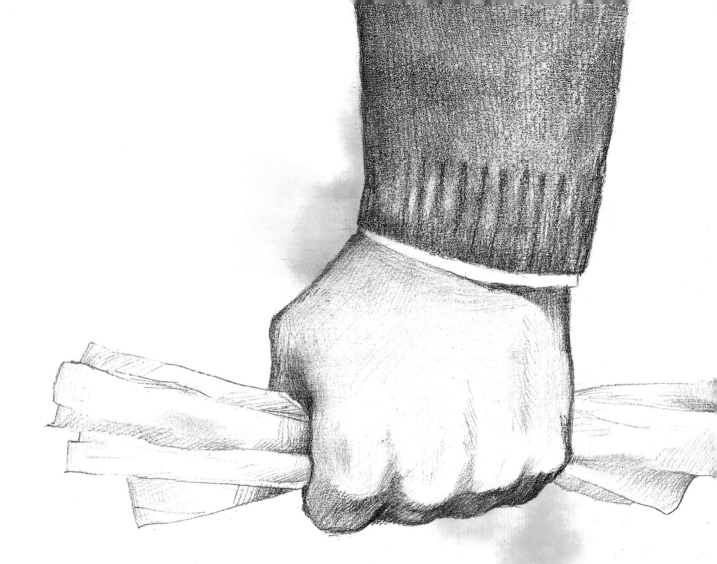

Tu Shou'e peacefully accepted this huge challenge. He said, "I don't believe there is something that others can do, but that we can't." The team decided to complete the whole project on their own. Decades later, Tu had already achieved great success as a lead scientist in China. He said during an interview: "When you see a problem, you solve it. You will eventually know how to do it all. There is nothing ready-made in the world."

The process of developing the missile was not smooth. China's first medium and short-range missile crashed in its first flight test. All members of the research group were very sad and disappointed, but they did not let this failure defeat them. Tu Shou'e and his colleagues began their research again.

After two years of hard work, China's self-designed medium and short-range missile flight test was successful. After that, Tu Shou'e was appointed as the chief designer for developing China's first long-range missile. But soon, a national political crisis stopped the missile development work once more.

However, nothing could stop Tu from moving forward. He paid no attention except for collecting research materials and blueprints. He continued to visit experts, raise innovative ideas, and search for breakthroughs in his research. During this chaotic time, Tu made incredible progress in his work. In September 1971, China's first long-range missile completed its half-range flight test successfully.

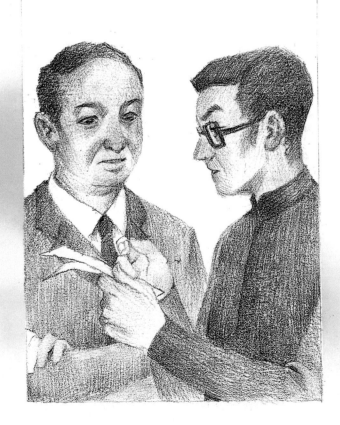

Tu Shou'e knew there was still a long way to go: they must complete the full-range flight test in order to put the missile into use. But this goal seemed impossible under such political turmoil, and the project that carried so many people's hopes and devotion had to be put off indefinitely.

They must wait, even though they were so close to success.
They waited nine years for an opportunity to rise.

Finally, in 1980, the project restarted. Tu Shou'e led the test team into the desert. For days and nights, they traveled back and forth in the harsh environment, checking the complicated cables and wires over and over again to make sure the test was safe.

This experiment was of great significance
to everyone; there must be no mistakes.

21

Tu Shou'e was over 60 years old at that time, but he insisted on climbing the tens of meters high launch tower to make the final inspection before the launch.

"We made it!!" cheers broke out in the crowd when it was announced on the news that the missile had successfully hit its target. Among the smiling faces, Tu broke into tears like a child.

"We will do whatever the country asks for." Tu Shou'e's motto motivated him to change his study from aviation to aerospace, and devote himself to China's aerospace industry. For decades, he worked hard in his job, and he spent his weekend afternoons with many others at Qian Xuesen's home to study or discuss technical problems.[1]

In 1998, he donated 300,000 RMB of his private savings to the Beihang University to set up the "Hongzhi Qinghan Financial Aid" in support of poor students. In many ways, Tu contributed to aerospace development by showing his enthusiasm and hope for China's future aerospace industry.

---

[1] Qian Xuesen was a world's famous scientist and one of the founders of dynamics studies in modern China. In China, he has been known many names such as "the Father of China's Aerospace Industry," "the Father of China's Missile Program," "the Father of Auto-control Science," and "the King of Rocketry."

His dedication helped him achieve extraordinary things in his career. Together, Tu Shou'e, Ren Xinmin, Huang Weilu, and Liang Shoupan are revered as the "four patriarchs of aerospace" in China.

About the Authors

Ye Qiang studied oil paintings at Sichuan Fine Arts Institute. After graduating in 2001, he began teaching as an associate professor in the department of New Media Art and Design at Beihang University. Ye's paintings have been displayed in hundreds of national and international exhibitions, and he has held solo exhibitions in galleries, including the Shanghai Art Museum, several times. Ye's paintings and scholarship can be found in more than 20 academic journals and monographs. He has also published seven textbooks.

Dong Pingping is Vice-Secretary of the Party Committee and a member of the Supervisory Commission of the department of New Media Art and Design at Beijing University of Aeronautics and Astronautics.

Figures in China's Space Industry:
Who is Tu Shou'e?

Written by Ye Qiang and Dong Pingping

First published in 2023 by Royal Collins Publishing Group Inc.
Groupe Publication Royal Collins Inc.
BKM Royalcollins Publishers Private Limited

Headquarters: 550-555 boul. René-Lévesque O Montréal (Québec) H2Z1B1 Canada
India office: 805 Hemkunt House, 8th Floor, Rajendra Place, New Delhi 110 008

Original Edition © Shaanxi People's Education Press Co., Ltd.

ISBN: 978-1-4878-1109-9

To find out more about our publications, please visit www.royalcollins.com.